HOW TO OUTLINE A COZY MYSTERY

Sara Rosett

Sign up for Sara's newsletter at www.SaraRosett.com

Cover: Inspired Cover Designs

HOW TO OUTLINE A COZY MYSTERY

Sara Rosett

INTRODUCTION

Cozy mystery readers are a voracious bunch. They love their cozies, and they want more of them. If you want to write a cozy, this workbook will help you create a plan to get your words down on paper.

The *How to Outline a Cozy Mystery Workbook* is a companion to the *How to Outline a Cozy Mystery Course*. The online course provides visual illustrations and more in-depth detail, especially in the sections about Classic Plot Structure and how the cozy fits into that structure. Within the course, I provide questions at the end of each section to help you create your own cozy mystery outline. You'll find those questions listed here in this companion workbook plus additional questions to help you dig deeper as you outline your cozy.

I've been writing and publishing for ten years, both in the traditional publishing world as well as in the indie, or self-publishing, world. I put together the *How to Outline a Cozy Mystery Course* and the *How to Outline a Cozy Mystery Workbook* to pass along what I've learned and help aspiring cozy writers understand the structure of a cozy as well as the genre itself.

Who is this workbook for?

If you want to write a cozy, this workbook is definitely for you, but there are a few other groups of people who will find it helpful.

If you write in another genre and want to layer mystery elements into your story, this workbook will give you the basic elements of a mystery, and you can apply those elements to your subplot.

If you are a beginning writer and you're interested in learning the basics of story structure, this workbook will give you a good foundation in the basic building blocks of a plot.

Now let's get started!

OUTLINING VS. "PANTSING"

Some writers write by the seat of their pants. "Pantsers" dive in and begin writing perhaps with only a few ideas, a character, a situation, or a setting. They put their fingers on the keyboard and let the story take them.

For me, writing by the seat of my pants is terrifying. I don't like writing that way. I want to have some idea of where I'm going in the story, some guideposts or landmarks, along the way. In short, I want a plan. That plan is my outline.

The word *outline* is a loaded term and can have negative connotations for people because it conjures up images of Roman numerals and indents and rigid structure. When I use the word *outline* I'm not talking about an outline like we learned about in school, which is probably good news to most of you. I'm pretty sure that most people don't think of their novels in a way that would fit into a traditional outline.

So what do we mean when we talk about outlining?

The good news is that there are many types of outlines, or plans, you can use to lay out the structure of your story. In fact, instead of using the word *outline*, a better term is probably *method*. The definition of *method* from my handy built-in Scrivener dictionary is: "a particular form of procedure for accomplishing or approaching something, especially a systematic or established one."

So an outlining method is whatever form or procedure you use to organize your thoughts about your cozy.

You can use any type of outlining method that works for you. You can use any combination of outlining methods that you want. I've found it helpful to use different outlining methods when I'm working on different sections of the book. And I've also found that my outlining methods have changed over the years.

In short, there are no right or wrong ways to outline your novel.

Most popular outlining methods:

Synopsis—a narrative summary of the story, usually two or three pages long

Note Cards—each chapter or even each scene is listed on a separate card (sometimes sticky notes are used instead of notecards)

List—a simple list of events is a basic outline

Mind map—this is a more visual and free-form way of representing the story

Grid—allows you to see all the major plot points on a single sheet of paper

For visual examples of these outlining methods, see the *Kinds of Outlines* module in the *How to Outline a Cozy Mystery* course.

Which outlining method should you use?

The best way to figure out which method of outlining works best for you is to try them. Experiment and see which is helpful. When I began writing I used a combination of a mind map and a written synopsis. I didn't use a grid. Now I use mostly a grid and mind maps along with a few lists thrown in.

Questions to help you think about the outlining method that might work best for you:

- Are you a detail person? (Try note cards or sticky notes)

- Do you like to have an overview of the situation? (Try the grid or mind map)

- Are you a visual learner? Do you like to sketch and doodle? (Try mind maps)

- Are you a list-maker? (Try the list method)

- Does telling stories verbally come naturally to you? (Try the synopsis method, perhaps even dictating it.

Which types of outlining methods have you used before? (Not necessarily for writing, but in any area of your life.)

Which type of outlining method listed above resonates with you?

How do you organize your daily tasks, either at work or home, and how could you apply that method to planning your novel?

Difference Between Mysteries and Thrillers

Mysteries and thrillers are often lumped together and called crime fiction, but there are some very sharp differences between the two genres, and it's important to understand those differences. When a reader picks up a mystery (or a book that *looks* like a mystery because of the cover and description), they expect certain things. If the reader doesn't find those things in the book, they'll be unhappy, which can mean that they might leave a one-star review of the book because it disappointed them. And it can also mean they won't read your next book, so it's very important to know what reader expectations are for mysteries. One of the best ways to illustrate what readers want is to compare and contrast mysteries and thrillers.

The Mind Game vs. The Thrill Ride

Mysteries have a puzzle at the core of the story. The book is a mind game between the reader and the author.

The reader tries to figure out who the killer is before the author reveals it at the end of the book. Mysteries usually have a closed community of suspects. Clues and red herrings are vital to the story. The antagonist is not revealed until the end. The main question is *whodunit*?

Interestingly, thrillers have a counterpoint, an opposite, in almost every area. Thrillers are a thrill ride with dramatic highs and lows, usually with a quick-paced storyline. Unlike a mystery, which usually has a closed setting that creates a small community, the setting of a thriller is often wide-ranging, and can even be globe-trotting. The emphasis is on the action, not the clues. The antagonist is often known, and readers may experience part of the story through the antagonist's point of view. Thrillers usually have a ticking clock, and the story question isn't whodunit, but *how to stop it?*

Mysteries are more cerebral with their emphasis on the puzzle while thrillers are more action-oriented. Mysteries tend to fit into episodic television well because of their closed community and their tightly focused story question of whodunit? Shows like *Elementary, Castle, Bones, The Mentalist, Death in Paradise*, the BBC's version of *Sherlock*, and the *CSI* franchise all adhere to the basic mystery structure.

The heightened drama, quick pace, and larger scope of thrillers mean that they translate into feature films more easily. *The Bourne Identity, The Da Vinci Code,* and *The Silence of the Lambs* are examples of thrillers from the big screen.

You can have thriller elements in your mystery, but

keep in mind the core type of story that a mystery reader wants as you plan your book.

Things to Consider Related to the Difference Between Mysteries and Thrillers:

What are your favorite mysteries (on the page as well as on the screen)?

What are your favorite thrillers (books and movies)?

What do you expect when you pick up a mystery?

Think about the last mystery you read that disappointed you. Why were you unsatisfied?

MYSTERY READER EXPECTATIONS

Now that we've looked at the larger differences between mysteries and thrillers, let's break down reader expectations a bit more with a focus on three key aspects that readers expect in their mysteries.

Mystery Readers Want "Fair Play"

The reader pits himself against the author to figure out whodunit before the murderer is revealed. The reader must have all the clues. One sure way to tick off mystery readers is to have your sleuth find a clue but never describe the clue to the reader. If you do that, you've broken trust with the mystery reader, essentially robbing the reader of the chance to outwit you. It's like playing a card game with a card up your sleeve. We'll talk more about how to hide clues and use red herrings later on. For now, just realize that the clues are a vital aspect of the story to a mystery reader, and you have to give the reader all the clues.

Mystery Readers Want All the Suspects Introduced Early in the Novel

Not only must the reader know all the clues, all the suspects must be there as well. Introduce the murderer early. Don't pop him/her in during the last few scenes of the book like a magician producing a rabbit from a hat. It's related to fair play. If you don't give readers a fair chance to solve the crime themselves, they will be upset.

How early is early enough? It will vary with each book, but I'd say that you should have all your suspects introduced within the first few chapters. At the latest, make sure it is before the end of Act One. More on that later as well.

Justice Must Be Done

Agatha Christie compared the mystery novel to medieval morality plays. Good triumphs over evil. Justice is done. A line from the movie *The Mummy* sums up the attitude of mystery readers nicely. Evelyn, the librarian, is speaking to a greedy, lying, and manipulative character when she says, "You know, nasty little fellows such as yourself always get their comeuppance."

The murderer's comeuppance can take many forms. The most common is arrest and punishment, but suicide or even the death of the murderer can provide the restoration of balance that readers want. At the end of the mystery novel, the equilibrium of the community is restored.

Things to Consider Related to Mystery Reader Expectations:

What clues will you include in the book that will reveal the true killer?

How will you make sure that all your suspects are introduced early in the book?

How will justice be done? How will your antagonist get his/her comeuppance?

How will balance be restored to the community?

PROTAGONIST

Now that you know what mystery readers expect in general, let's drill down another level and focus on the conventions of cozy mysteries. These elements are the basic building blocks of your mystery. We'll look at these essential elements through the lens of what cozy readers want and expect. This is the point where we dip into the psychology behind what cozy readers are looking for. We'll look at not only the elements themselves, but why these elements are so compelling to cozy readers. I've heard these elements described as catnip to readers. Whether it is a certain type of protagonist or setting or any of the other elements, these are the things that when a cozy reader hears about them, or reads about them in the book description, she thinks, "Oh, I want to read that."

Protagonist

There are exceptions to every rule, but in cozies, the protagonist is usually:

Female—Some cozies have a male protagonist, but not many. The majority of cozy readers are women, and they like to read about women.

An amateur sleuth—The protagonist of a cozy is not in professional law enforcement. Cozy readers don't want an in-depth look at police procedure. They want to explore the situation where an ordinary person is caught up in extraordinary circumstances.

Something interesting—This "something interesting" can be anything. It's called a hook, a way to hook the reader or catch their attention. A hook has another function, too. It's a great way to promote your book because it is something that sets your cozy apart from other books of the genre and makes your book unique.

Has family or friends around her—Cozy mysteries usually have a strong theme of family and friendship. The protagonist in a cozy isn't a lone wolf. She has quirky friends or crazy relatives that she interacts with throughout the novel. Begin thinking about the supporting characters. It is often through these supporting characters that the protagonist gets vital information about the investigation. Many cozies have a romantic subplot and the love interest(s) are part of the supporting characters.

We'll also cover supporting characters in more depth, but for now begin to think about the people who surround your protagonist.

Kinds of Hooks

Your hook might be an interesting or unusual job, which can be anything from archeologist to scuba diving instructor. I use the interesting job hook in my Ellie Avery series, which is about a professional organizer as well as in my Murder on Location series, which is about a location scout.

A hook can also be a hobby or an interest that your protagonist has or becomes interested in during the course of the book. Many cozies begin with a protagonist inheriting a business like a knitting shop or a bakery. Other times, the hobby or craft is new to the protagonist, and her growing interest and involvement in it becomes the hook of the story. Reading about these interests and hobbies are vicarious wish fulfillment for cozy readers. They enjoy experiencing these hobbies or activities along with the character whether or not they practice those specific activities themselves. Many readers of knitting mysteries love to knit, but those books also have readers who don't knit and only want to experience the hobby through the book.

Recently, cozy mysteries have become synonymous with hobby and craft interests, and while readers love experiencing these activities vicariously, hobbies weren't always so closely associated with the genre. You don't have to have a craft or hobby theme for your cozy.

If a cozy hook with a craft or hobby theme appeals to you, make sure that you figure out how to make your cozy stand out in a crowded market. There are plenty of culinary cozies right now. If you want to write one of these, you'll need to differentiate your cozy from all the other food-themed cozies.

Your hook might also be the protagonist's residence. Cozy readers love cute small towns and cozy villages, so those settings are often hooks. However, if you're using the setting as a hook it doesn't necessarily have to be a small town. If your protagonist lives in a lighthouse or a genteel Victorian mansion or in a swanky high-rise, those could all be an interesting hooks to draw in readers. We'll explore setting more in the next section.

Things to Think About Related to Your Protagonist:

What is it about your protagonist that is interesting/different?

How is your protagonist an amateur when it comes to the investigation?

If you plan to write a cozy with a craft or hobby theme, how will you make your cozy stand out in a crowded market?

Who are your protagonist's friends/family?

Will family or friends help the protagonist get information about the investigation?

If your cozy has a romantic subplot, how will the love interest be part of your protagonist's circle?

SETTING AND TONE

Setting and tone are so important to cozy mystery readers that I've listed them right after the protagonist in the catalogue of essential elements.

Setting

The setting of a cozy needs to be a closed community. The focus of a cozy is on whodunit, and you want a small group of potential suspects. The closed community is often a small town or village, but it doesn't have to be limited to those types of areas. The closed community can be a snowbound train, a neighborhood, a workplace, or a school. In my Ellie books, Ellie is a military spouse, and the military base is often the closed community. In another book in that series, the closed community is an island resort.

Tone

The other important thing to remember about setting involves tone. Cozy mystery readers want to read about a place they want to go: a cute town or seaside B&B resort, not a rat-infested, abandoned nuclear power plant. That's an extreme example, but it does illustrate the point. *Cozy* is the keyword here. Cozy readers don't want to read about "the mean streets." *Appealing* and *fun* are words you should be able to use to describe your setting, not grim or gritty.

If your setting is grim or gritty, it might be too dark for cozy readers. Cozy readers love getting to know a setting and returning to it again and again—just like they love learning more about the friends, family, and community around the protagonist. And they want the setting to be a place they'd like to visit personally.

World-building

Creating a cozy setting with the right tone takes a lot of work. It involves world-building, which is a term usually more associated with science fiction and fantasy writers, but it is critical for cozy writers. While we aren't creating new planets or imaginary worlds, the world of the cozy is extremely important and needs to be detailed.

In the Ellie books, I have to know the streets of Ellie's neighborhood and the different areas of town as well as the military base. In the Murder on Location books, I have to know the English village and the surrounding countryside.

Things to Consider About Setting and ⌐

What is the setting of your cozy?

How is it enclosed?

Does your protagonist fit in or not? Special knowledge of the closed community is often the motivation for investigating.

How is the setting cozy? Will readers want to return to it again because they want to get away to that same sort of locale?

What is the tone of your story? Is it light enough for a cozy?

ANTAGONIST

Your antagonist must be part of the closed community—it's that fair play thing again. And he or she must be introduced early in the book so your reader has a chance to consider the character as a possibility for being the killer.

In a mystery there is less emphasis on the antagonist than in a thriller. In a thriller, the reader often knows the identity of the antagonist, and the reader may see some of the story through the antagonist's point of view.

In contrast, in a mystery the antagonist usually isn't known until the end of the story when the killer is revealed. I like to layer in a few clues to the true personality of the antagonist throughout the story so that readers have a hint of foreshadowing about the antagonist —not a lot, but a few. Those hints might be that the person lies or cheats, or it might be that they have a secret, or they might blackmail someone. It can be a seemingly small incident in the story, like belittling their spouse or children.

Motive of the Antagonist

Another aspect of your antagonist that is vital to mystery readers is that he or she have a real motive. The explanation that the antagonist was mentally unhinged is not what mystery readers want. They want a motive rooted in real life like greed or lust.

Some motives are obvious and easy to understand like blackmail, greed, and lust. Other motives like justice and revenge are harder to understand, and may require a little more explanation to make it believable.

Things to Consider Related to Your Antagonist:

How is your antagonist part of the community?

When is he/she introduced? (Make it early!)

What is his/her motivation? Is it "big" enough?

Will the reader believe a person would commit murder for this reason?

If not, how can you make it significant enough?

MURDER

One of the hallmarks of a cozy mystery is the lack of graphic violence. Cozy readers want to escape gruesome violence, not experience it firsthand.

So how do you write a book about murder but keep it cozy? You don't linger on the graphic nature of the crime. Usually, you keep the death off-stage.

Cozies as "Clean Books"

Besides being less graphic when it comes to violence, cozies are usually "clean" books, which means they have limited language and sex. There are exceptions to every rule, but in general, cozy readers want a book without a lot of swearing or graphic violence. If the book has a romantic element, readers usually want the romance to be secondary to the mystery plot. Books in the romantic suspense category flip these elements: the romance is the primary plot and the mystery is the subplot.

The Murder Method Itself

You might wonder if cozy readers are particular when it comes to the murder itself. If they want the gruesomeness of the death offstage, do you have to limit the murder method to poison or a nearly bloodless death through a neat stabbing or single gunshot? Surprisingly, the answer is no. As long as you don't linger on the graphic elements of the death, it can be as odd or unusual as you like.

Things to Think About Related to the Murder in your Cozy:

What is the murder method?

Was it premeditated or a prime of passion?

Does that fit with the murderer's character?

Do you need to research the murder method? If so, how will you make sure you don't get bogged down in research too long?

VICTIM AND SUSPECTS

The victim and the suspects in a cozy mystery will be drawn from the closed community around the protagonist. Unlike a police procedural where the investigators can go directly to suspects and question them immediately, you have to have a reason or motivation for your protagonist to question the suspects and a connection that enables your protagonist to do this.

Motivation and Connection

Motivation to Investigate—Most people stay far away from criminal investigations, so your protagonist needs a strong motivation. Often the protagonist's connection to the victim plays a role in getting the protagonist involved in the investigation. Reasons to get involved could range from the protagonist finding the victim to a special relationship that the protagonist had with the victim. The protagonist or someone close to her may be a suspect as well. But there are lots of other reasons you could use. Perhaps the protagonist unintentionally throws a friend under suspicion. Perhaps the protagonist knows the police are on the wrong track, which is an especially strong motive to get involved if the police focus on the protagonist as the main suspect, and she knows she didn't do it! Whatever motivation you use to get your protagonist involved, make sure it is a strong and compelling reason.

Connection—You also have to think about the relationships among the characters that will give your protagonist an entry into other people's lives to talk with them or to snoop on them.

When I'm thinking about suspects and the victim I use a mind map to get all my thoughts down on paper. I put the victim's name in the middle of the page. Then I surround the name of the victim with all the possible people who could have a motive to commit the murder. This method helps me visualize all the different relationships and how the different characters' lives intersect with each other.

One of the challenges of writing a cozy is bringing all the characters together. Often the closed setting will help you with this aspect of plotting: all the characters work in the same office or live in the same neighborhood or are members of the same club. Other times, when the suspects are more loosely connected I'll use an event to bring the characters together like a school program or a family reunion.

Discovering Suspects

Next, consider how your protagonist will discover someone is a suspect. As an amateur, your protagonist won't have access to physical evidence in the case, which is often how a detective in a police procedural discovers suspects. Finding out someone is a suspect is another big hurdle for cozy mystery writers, but there are lots of ways to handle it.

Some suspects will be obvious right away. If someone had a conflict with the victim, then they're usually a suspect. Or a character may be seen leaving the scene of the crime.

Other suspects will be less obvious, and your protagonist will have to work harder to discover these suspects. Engaging in blackmail, threats, or lies are all usually hidden from the protagonist, at least initially, and you'll have to figure out how your protagonist discovers these less obvious suspects.

Suspects' Reactions

Finally, consider how your suspects will react to your protagonist's questions. Again, a sleuth in a cozy isn't a law enforcement professional, so your protagonist will have to find ways to get information. No one has to answer her questions. Consider why a suspect would be willing to talk to your protagonist. Reasons can be as diverse as a character wanting to show off their inside knowledge, a desire to get someone in trouble, or a character may have a guilty conscience and want to unburdened themselves.

Things to Think About Related to Suspects and the Victim:

Why is your protagonist driven to ask questions and find answers?

How will your protagonist connect with the different suspects?

Do you need some event or situation that brings all the suspects together?

How will your protagonist discover suspects?

Why will suspects answer your protagonist's questions?

How will your suspects' reactions to the protagonist reveal their character?

VISIBLE/INVISIBLE STORYLINES

All novels are formed of plots and subplots, intertwining layers of stories. In a mystery, in addition to any subplots you have, you have two very different layers to the story. The first layer is what I think of as the visible storyline. It is what is happening on the surface, moment by moment, with your protagonist and other characters. Examples of visible storyline elements are the discovery of the body, discovering suspects, pursuing clues, and interviewing suspects.

The other layer of the story is the invisible storyline, which is what is going on under the surface. Examples of the invisible storyline include the actual murder, the actions the murderer takes to cover his or her tracks, and the red herrings.

The invisible storyline may pop up and become visible momentarily throughout the story. We may get a glimpse of the murderer's true character, or we may see a clue that points to the solution to the mystery, but for the most part the invisible storyline is not revealed until the very end of the book when the murderer is revealed and the clues are sorted from the red herrings. At that point, the truth is known about what really happened, not what we *thought* happened.

I find it helpful to have two different timelines when I'm working on a book. I have the main storyline of what is happening to my protagonist and the characters around her—that's the visible storyline. And then I have the hidden, or invisible, storyline of what the murderer is doing.

Things to Think About Regarding Visible and Invisible Storylines:

What are the visible elements of your storyline?

What are the invisible elements of your storyline?

When might the invisible become visible for a moment?

What will your antagonist do to keep his or her actions invisible?

THREE ESSENTIALS TO GET STARTED

We've covered a lot of information in the section on the basic elements. I know it can be overwhelming, so I thought it would be helpful to condense things down to the three most basic elements you need to get started with your cozy mystery.

Make sure you know who the victim is, who the murderer is, and what the murder method is.

If you have those three things, you have the basis for your invisible storyline and can build the visible storyline on top of it.

Three Basic Things to Get Started:

Who is the victim?

Who is the murderer (the antagonist)?

What is the murder method?

ACT I

Almost all stories have a structure that is surprisingly similar. Over the years, people have deconstructed this framework, breaking it into parts and analyzing each section. The structure of stories is sometimes called the Classic Plot Structure, the Hero's Journey, or the Three-Act Structure.

We'll keep our analysis of plot structure brief and high-level—a bird's-eye view—but if you want more in-depth detail there are plenty of good resources on this subject. I'll give you a list of my favorite plot and structure books in the *Resources* section at the end of the workbook.

A quick note on terminology. Most stories can be divided into four parts, but story structure is often called the Three-Act Structure with the second act divided into Part A and Part B. So you'd refer to the second section of the story as Act Two Part A. Very confusing for me and for you! So I'll refer to each section as a separate act: Acts —One, Two, Three, and Four.

In the *How to Outline a Cozy Mystery Course*, I go into detail and use two different movies, *Murder on the Orient Express* and *Rear Window*, to give in-depth examples of each act, but I won't go into such depth for this workbook. We'll keep our focus on applying the concepts to your story. For more details and examples of how story structure works, check out the course's module on plot structure as well as the separate modules on Act One, Act Two, Act Three, and Act Four.

Act One

Act One is your introduction. I like to have a simplified name for each act. It helps me keep in mind the function of that act and keeps me on track. I think of Act One as the Ordinary World.

In Act One, you meet the protagonist and find out what they want (their internal and external goals or desires). You experience the setting, and you get the setup (the story situation). In *Rear Window*, the story setup is a bored photographer stuck in his apartment with his leg in a cast, watching his neighbors. In *Murder on the Orient Express*, the story setup is that Poirot overhears a suspicious conversation and a man traveling on the same train has had death threats.

In Act One you also meet the supporting cast. You may also have what James Scott Bell in his book *Plot and Structure* calls a "disturbance" in Act One. It is usually an event that foreshadows the coming Turning Point. The disturbance is not as dramatic as the Turning Point, but it lets readers know something isn't quite right. In *Murder on the Orient Express*, the disturbance is the suspicious conversation that Poirot overhears. You don't have to have a disturbance, but you do need a Turning Point.

At the end of Act One, something happens that launches the protagonist into the rest of the story. The protagonist faces a challenge, hurdle, struggle, or task that forms the central question as well as the rest of the action of the story. This "something" that happens is the first Turning Point of the story. In a mystery, the classic Act One Turning Point is the discovery of the body.

That's a lot of work for your story to do in one Act, so let's break down each aspect of Act One.

Meet the Protagonist

What is your protagonist's ordinary world?

How will you introduce your protagonist? How will that introduction show her character and her place in the ordinary world?

What does your protagonist want? What is her external goal? What is her desire?

What is your protagonist's internal goal or desire? Does she have one?

What is in opposition to those goals?

Setting

What is the setting of the book?

How is it cozy?

Supporting Characters

How do you introduce the supporting characters?

If you have a large group of supporting characters, how will you stagger their introductions so you don't overwhelm the reader?

How will each introduction of the supporting characters reveal his or her character?

Story Setup

What is the story setup? What situation is the story born out of?

Disturbance

Do you have a disturbance in Act One? Do you need one?

S Rosett

Turning Point

What is the Turning Point of Act One?

If your Act One Turning Point is not the discovery of the body, is it compelling enough to propel your protagonist onto a new path and into a New World in Act Two?

How does the Turning Point change everything for your protagonist and launch her onto a new path?

ACT II

New World of the Investigation

In Act Two, your protagonist enters a New World. In a cozy mystery, the New World is the world of the investigation. The protagonist develops a plan to deal with the challenge, which in the case of a mystery is usually to find the killer. The protagonist makes the decision to investigate and begins to discover suspects and interview them. (However, like most things related to plot structure, the decision to investigate is flexible. It can also occur during Act One. Or it may even be the Turning Point of Act One.) During Act Two the protagonist usually develops a theory about who committed the crime.

Reactive

My single word identifier for Act Two is Reactive. The protagonist is pursuing the goal, but only halfheartedly. Often the protagonist is being pushed around by the antagonist. Usually at this point in a mystery, a couple of things are emphasized: there is a determination that the death wasn't random and the suspect pool is narrowed to the small group, the closed community.

Try/Fail Cycles

As you move through Act Two and Act Three, the main focus of action in a cozy is the identification of suspects in the closed community and the questioning of the suspects. But if you have your protagonist interview one person after another, your reader will get bored. Your story needs a pattern, an ebb and flow of rising and falling action that will keep readers interested and wondering what will happen next. Usually your protagonist will float a theory or suggest a perpetrator, but they will be wrong. Then they'll do it again, and fail again.

This pattern is the Try/Fail Cycle that keeps readers turning pages. The Try/Fail Cycle runs through both Act Two and Act Three, but it is handled differently in each act so that there is gradually increasing tension and bigger and bigger stakes. In Act Two, usually your protagonist makes their first halfhearted attempt to solve the crime and fails.

Keeping Promises to the Reader

Act Two is also the act where you begin to fulfill promises you've made to the reader. Blake Snyder in his book *Save the Cat* calls this part of the story the "Fun and Games" section. If you've told readers your book will be a cozy about a chef, this section of the book should have your protagonist in the kitchen whipping up some delicious recipes. In my book *Death in the English Countryside*, I promise readers a look at a quaint English village, and in Act Two, Kate explores the village from the inn to the pub to the stately home outside the village. If you promise a funny cozy, make sure Act Two has humor in it.

Turning Point or Midpoint

At the end of this section is the next Turning Point, sometimes called the Midpoint because it is in the middle of your story. The Act Two Turning Point in a mystery is often a second dead body—and if it is the person who was your protagonist's main suspect, it makes a great reversal. Your protagonist will have tried and failed and will have to reassess everything.

Things to Think About Related to Act Two:

How does the New World of the investigation impact the protagonist?

How does the protagonist's view of friends/family change because of the investigation? Are any friends or family suspects? Is the protagonist a suspect?

What reason does the protagonist have to investigate?

How is it established that the crime wasn't random violence?

How is the suspect pool narrowed to the closed community?

How is the protagonist pursuing her goal to solve the case, but only halfheartedly?

How is the antagonist pushing the protagonist around at this stage?

How does the protagonist try and fail in Act Two?

What is the Turning Point of Act Two?

ACT III

Act Three is similar to Act Two (suspects, clues, and theories are all in play), but Act Three is like Act Two on steroids. Your protagonist has a bigger plan, bigger goals, and a bigger risk of failure. The stakes are higher than they have ever been. Your protagonist can't go back from this point. She's totally invested, and now she takes control. The single word I use to describe Act Three is Proactive. At the end of this act is the last reveal—the biggest, most dramatic discovery that sends the story hurtling toward the inevitable confrontation and conclusion.

The final Turning Point may be a clue that causes everything to fall into place, such as a piece of physical evidence. Or it may be an action or an avoidance of action that indicates guilt. In *Rear Window*, it's Thorwald's inaction that indicates his guilt. He continues to smoke in the dark instead of going to the window when the dog owner screams, drawing everyone's attention.

All Is Lost Moment

Your protagonist reaches a point in the Try/Fail cycle that is called the "All is Lost" moment when it seems impossible that she will solve the crime. Act Three is also the point when the antagonist usually strikes again. Since your protagonist won't give up—she can't at this point—the antagonist has to pull out all the stops to force her to quit. Sometimes this attack is an attempt on the protagonist's life.

Some Suspects Cleared at This Point

As your protagonist moves through Act Three, some suspects will be cleared, which is part of the Try/Fail Cycle. Questions are answered and some suspects have alibis. These dead ends for your protagonist are actually a positive. They allow you to clear up some questions before the final scenes of the book. You don't want to have seven or eight suspects to deal with at the end of the novel. Too many unresolved suspects can get a little unwieldy—unless you're Agatha Christie!

Things to Think About Related to Act Three:

How do things become even more serious in Act Three? How are the stakes raised?

How is your protagonist fully invested now?

What is the Try/Fail cycle for your protagonist in Act Three? How do her attempts and failures get bigger?

What is the "all is lost" moment?

How is the antagonist upping his/her game during Act Three?

What suspects are cleared at this point?

What is the Turning Point of Act Three that sets the final conflict in motion?

ACT IV

Act Four is the final confrontation. Your entire novel has been building to this point. Everything comes together, and often with the worst possible outcomes—at least temporarily. At the end of Act Four, the killer has been unmasked, the murder method is revealed (if it's not already known), the killer gets his or her comeuppance, and equilibrium is restored to the community. Then we usually get a final glimpse of the characters at the conclusion of the book.

Final Confrontation

In Golden Age fiction, Act Four usually meant all the suspects gathered in one place, and the sleuth revealing the truth. That scenario rarely happens in today's mystery fiction. Usually, Act Four is a battle—either a battle of wits with the protagonist tricking the antagonist into a confession, or the battle may be an actual physical fight.

Often the worst thing that could happen is what takes place.

In *Rear Window*, Thorwald discovers Lisa in his apartment, then realizes Jeff has been watching him, and then Thorwald goes to Jeff's apartment, where Jeff is alone and can't defend himself because he's stuck in a wheelchair.

A physical confrontation is the final battle in *Rear Window*, with Thorwald winning momentarily as he pushes Jeff out the window, but the police arrive and arrest Thorwald. Despite Jeff seeming to lose the final battle, he's actually won because the conflict has revealed that Thorwald is a killer.

Unique Tools and Skills

In the final battle, your protagonist needs to use her unique tools and skills to defend herself. Jeff uses his camera and flashbulbs in *Rear Window*. Poirot uses his "little gray cells." In my Ellie books, Ellie has used things out of her diaper bag as well as her knowledge of the military squadron in the final battle. Whatever it is that your protagonist uses, make sure it is set up before. If your protagonist will use a gun in the final battle make sure you mention it before that scene. If it's a knowledge of handwriting or a martial arts move, make sure it is set up in earlier chapters.

Getting to the Final Confrontation in a Cozy

Reaching the final confrontation in a cozy can be a challenge. Like most people avoid criminal investigations, most people avoid criminals and would not approach a potential murderer and confront them with evidence proving they committed a crime. Don't have your protagonist do something that would be idiotic. In short, don't let her be "too stupid to live."

One way to handle getting to the final confrontation in a cozy is to have your protagonist make the final discovery at a point where the antagonist is present and realizes that your protagonist knows the truth, which will bring about the confrontation. The protagonist *must* deal with the antagonist before she can give the information to the police. Another way to handle the confrontation in a cozy is to have the antagonist confront the protagonist.

Avoid a Confession Monologue

During the final confrontation, avoid a long confession monologue, if possible. Criminals droning on for paragraphs about why and how they committed a crime tend to stretch a reader's suspension of disbelief. If you clear up either the motive or the method before the final confrontation scene, you won't have as much explanation to work into that final scene. It can be difficult to write the story in a way that it doesn't have a confession monologue, and I've certainly had to use them, but the more cozies I've written, the more I try to *not* to use them.

If you do have to have some explanation, use dialogue and keep it as limited as possible. Another possibility is to move some of the explanation to the final coda at the end of the book.

Final Coda

Readers like a last glimpse of the characters back in their ordinary world. Everything is back to normal, yet everything has changed. You can use this part of the story to explain any open questions and show the reader that the world is cozy again.

Things to Consider for Act Four:

What is the worst thing that could happen to your protagonist?

How will your protagonist confront the antagonist? Directly, or will she be forced into it...or even surprised by the antagonist?

What unique tools or skills will your protagonist use to win the battle?

Have those tools/skills been part of the story from the beginning?

How will justice be done?

How will equilibrium be restored to the community? And how will you show that in the final coda?

How will you wrap up the subplots and questions your reader might have?

What glimpse of your character's new world will you give the reader?

CREATIVITY

Some people think the words *structure* and *genre* are synonymous with cookie-cutter stories, but I think that story structure is the opposite. The basic elements of the story create a structure, an underpinning, that give you a framework to build on, but each element has many variations. As a result, you can have thousands of different outcomes, depending on how individual authors put their stories together.

Think of it this way: all houses have walls, doors, windows, bedrooms, living areas, and kitchens, but there are incredible variations in different designs and types of houses.

Story structure works the same way. Authors take the basic building blocks of protagonist, setting, clues, red herrings, etc. and combine them, even twist them and turn them in different ways, creating countless unique stories.

In the course, I give the example of the discovery of the body. Every murder mystery needs a body, but that element can be spun many different ways. Perhaps the body is missing and that's the mystery. Someone is missing from a cruise ship or a man doesn't return home from work one evening. Where is he? Sometimes the whole body isn't found—just a part, which sounds kind of gruesome for a cozy, but cozy readers will be okay with it if you don't linger on the gore of the discovery. Maybe there's too many bodies. I used this situation in *Magnolias, Moonlight, and Murder.* When a Civil-War-era cemetery is flooded and several coffins open, one contains two bodies, and one of those bodies was definitely of a modern person, not someone who died in a Civil War battle. Another take on the discovery of the body might be that the body is found but disappears, which brings up all sorts of questions for your protagonist, a situation I used in *Deception* as well as in *Mint Juleps, Mayhem, and Murder.* The bodies went missing in those two books for different reasons and each had a different impact on the storyline. As you can see from the example, just one element can give you many different options when it comes to plotting. Getting creative with each of the following elements is discussed in more depth in the *Creativity* module in the course.

Things to Think About As you Customize Story Elements in Unique Ways:

Do you think of story structure as rigid or flexible?

Which elements of story structure would you like to put a new spin on?

Now let's look at a few specific elements and consider how we can be creative with them.

Suspects

Everyone has something to hide, but not all secrets lead to murder. Some secrets are innocent secrets. People may be embarrassed about an activity or they simply may not be ready to share something with their friends or family, so they may act suspiciously, creating a situation where they *look* guilty. "Innocent secrets" are great for plotting those red herrings and filling up your protagonist's suspect list. They also result in dead ends, which are so important in the Try/Fail cycle.

What innocent secrets could your suspects be hiding?

What actions will they take that will make them look suspicious?

How will those actions make them depart from "normal story theory" as Erle Stanley Gardner would phrase it? In other words, in what way will their behavior be incongruent, or at odds, with their normal behavior?

Interviewing Suspects

To keep interviews interesting, set encounters between your protagonist and suspects on the suspect's "home turf."

How can you show each suspect in their natural element?

How can you show each suspect's personality and character through their actions and dialogue during the interview?

Creativity and Clues

What will the antagonist do to cover his or her tracks? (These actions will create red herrings for the police and reader.)

What obstacles/disruptions in plan will the antagonist face?

How will the antagonist deal with these problems?

How will you hide clues (the real ones!) creatively?

What red herrings will you, as the author (as opposed to the actions of the antagonist) leave to confuse the trail for the reader?

Bending the Rules

Christie certainly bent the rules when she had twelve killers working together, but she did leave clues indicating the outcome. And *Rear Window* doesn't strictly follow the rules either. It is more of a "how-done-it?" instead of a whodunit. Both these stories bend the rules, showing the incredible flexibility of the mystery structure.

The "rules" regarding what is acceptable in a cozy mystery are even looser today than they were in the Golden Age of crime fiction when Christie wrote *Murder on the Orient Express*. You can have a much more significant romantic subplot to your book. You have some leeway on the amount of violence and language you use. You can even have paranormal elements or pet detectives. If your story contains a paranormal element or animal sleuth or something along those lines, make sure you are clear about it in your description so that readers will know what to expect.

If you're considering bending the rules in your cozy, how will you do it so that readers will still be satisfied?

How will you convey those differences to readers in your description?

WRITING A SERIES

Cozy readers love a series, so if you can shape your story idea into a series, readers will be happy. A series will benefit you as an author as well because readers will return again and again to the world you've created. But there are challenges associated with writing a series. Here are some possibilities for series arcs you'll want to consider if you plan to write a series. Keep in mind that you want to resolve the murder in each book. Leaving a murder mystery unresolved will leave your readers unsatisfied. Focus on other aspects of the series that can flow from book to book for series arcs.

Protagonist

What story arc(s) will the protagonist have that will

carry throughout the series, or through the first books in the series?

How will your protagonist grow or change?

Will the protagonist's arc be a long internal growth or will she face "smaller" more everyday challenges?

Will your protagonist's character flaws play into the series arc?

What external challenges (family relationships/ career/friendships) can be part of a series story arc?

Love Life

Often a series arc for a protagonist revolves around her love life. It is a great series arc that readers can get extremely invested in, but there are a few things to keep in mind in this area:

Which type of love life series arc will you use: will

they/won't they or love triangle?

If you use the will they/won't they, how will the story change if the two characters get together?

What are potential challenges and future story arcs if the two characters get together? Will they work together to solve future mysteries or not?

If you use the love triangle series arc, how will you resolve the arc? Who will she pick?

What can you do to foreshadow that outcome so that half your readers won't be upset?

After the love triangle is resolved, how do you see the two characters in the future of the series? Will they work together, or will the books still be a one-woman show with the love interest remaining a minor character?

Supporting Characters

Just as readers get involved in the protagonist's love life, they will also become invested in supporting characters.

What supporting characters will have strong series arcs?

Will those arcs be dramatic internal growth arcs or will they be more "everyday" challenges?

Do you see the other supporting characters

developing in later books so that they will "come into their own" as the series goes along? If so, which ones?

Could a supporting character become the protagonist in another book or series?

Setting

The setting itself can change and grow, impacting the series arcs.

How could the setting change over time?

Will growth and expansion impact the area where the story takes place, and thus the characters? Or could it be the opposite, a contraction in the local economy?

Will new characters arrive and somehow change the setting as well as the dynamics of the characters?

How can you exploit your setting? What different

areas can you write about in different books? What different regions of the setting would lend themselves to an in-depth exploration?

Will you take your series "on the road" occasionally? If you do leave your normal setting, how will you fulfill reader expectations during the book that is not in the normal setting?

How will you contrive to take some of the regular supporting characters on the road?

How will you keep the setting and tone cozy on the road?

WHERE TO START

We've just run through an incredible amount of information that can be overwhelming to process. I always feel a bit overwhelmed at the start of each book even though I know I've pulled it off many times. It still is a lot of elements to juggle.

The good news is that you don't have to have everything sorted and perfectly planned. If you focus on a few basic things, you can get started and fill in the rest as you go. Unless you are able to plan a whole book in one go. If you can do that—that's great! Go for it. If not, don't panic.

We've already gone over the basic aspects you need to get started—the bare bones of victim, murderer, and murder method—but if you want a plan that is a little more fleshed out, here are the expanded basics to get you started:

Who is your protagonist?

What is your setting?

Who is your antagonist?

Who are the suspects?

What are the clues that point to the identity of the killer?

What are the red herrings (either left by the killer or you, the author) to confuse the trail of clues?

What is the murder method?

Once you have your basic elements, rough out Act One of your story.

Ordinary world

Hint of evil/disturbance

Turning point to investigate

Motive to investigate

First theory your protagonist will pursue

First Turning Point

Then jot down the rest of the Turning Points at the end of Act Two and Act Three as well as what the final confrontation will be.

Act Two Turning Point

Act Three Turning Point

Final Confrontation

Conclusion

There—you've done it. You have a rough framework to build your story on. It's not complete, and it will change as you write, but you have a plan with some guideposts to get you from "Chapter One" to "The End."

I often start with this basic plan listed above. Once I have my basic elements and a rough outline of the turning points and the final confrontation, I begin writing. When I reach the end of Act One, I fill in the rest of Act Two and write that section, repeating as I move through the story. As I write, the middle and end of the story become clearer.

You may work in a completely opposite way and fill

in your whole story framework completely. Or you may fall somewhere in between.

Whatever system or method you use, the important thing is to get to the point where you can get the story down on paper. You can have the best outline or plan for a novel, but if you don't actually write it, no one will ever read it…so get to work! You've got readers out there waiting for another great cozy.

ADDITIONAL RESOURCES

Plot and Structure by James Scott Bell

Screenwriting Tricks for Authors by Alex Sokoloff

Save the Cat by Blake Snyder

Secrets of the World's Best-Selling Writer: The Storytelling Techniques of Erle Stanley Gardner by Francis L. and Roberta B. Fugate